Native Americans

The Navajo

Richard M. Gaines

ABDO Publishing Company

visit us at
www.abdopub.com

Published 2000
Printed in the United States of America
Second Printing 2002

Illustrator: David Fadden (pgs. 7, 11, 13, 17, 19, 21, 23, 25, 27)
Cover Photo: Corbis
Interior Photos: Corbis (pgs. 5, 9, 14, 15, 18, 20, 24, 28, 29, 30)
Editors: Bob Italia, Tamara L. Britton, Kate A. Furlong
Art Direction & Maps: Pat Laurel
Border Design: Carey Molter/MacLean & Tuminelly (Mpls.)

Library of Congress Cataloging-in-Publication Data

Gaines, Richard M., 1942-
    The Navajo / Richard M. Gaines.
        p. cm. -- (Native Americans)
    Includes bibliographical references and index.
    Summary: Presents a brief introduction to the Navajo Indians including information on their society, homes, food, clothing, crafts, and life today.
    ISBN 1-57765-374-2
    1. Navajo Indians--Juvenile literature. [1. Navajo Indians. 2. Indians of North America--Southwest, New.] I. Title.

E99.N3 G35 2000
979. 1'004972--dc21

                                                                    99-059870

Special thanks to Contributing Editor
IRVING NELSON, PROGRAM DIRECTOR
Office of Navajo Nation Library
Window Rock, Arizona

About the Illustrator: David Fadden

David Kanietakeron Fadden is a member of the Akwesasne Mohawk Wolf Clan. His work has appeared in publications such as *Akwesasne Notes, Indian Time*, and the *Northeast Indian Quarterly*. Examples of his work have also appeared in various publications of the Six Nations Indian Museum in Onchiota, NY. His work has also appeared in "How The West Was Lost: Always The Enemy," produced by Gannett Production which appeared on the Discovery Channel. David's work has been exhibited in Albany, NY; the Lake Placid Center for the Arts; Centre Strathearn in Montreal, Quebec; North Country Community College in Saranac Lake, NY; Paul Smiths College in Paul Smiths, NY; and at the Unison Arts & Learning Center in New Paltz, NY.

Contents

Homeland

Over a thousand years ago, the Navajo and their Apache relatives lived in northern Canada and Alaska. In A.D. 1000, they started moving south.

The Navajo Nation is in parts of Arizona, New Mexico, and Utah. It covers over 25,000 square miles (64, 750 sq k).

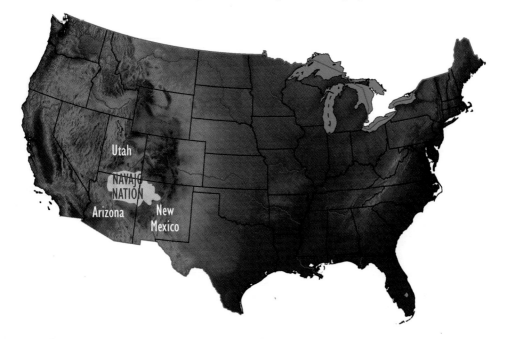

Some traveled east of the Rocky Mountains. Some went through present-day Nevada and Utah. Five hundred years later, they arrived in the deserts of northern New Mexico and Arizona. They decided to make the desert their new home.

The Navajo call themselves the "Dine." It means the "people." The Zuni, who already lived in the desert, called them the "apaches du nabahu." It means the "raiders of the field."

A Navajo girl in traditional dress stands on driftwood in front of the West Mitten butte. The butte is in Monument Valley, Arizona, which is within the Navajo Nation.

Society

The Navajo lived in groups of a few related families. The groups were spread over a wide area. They lived among neighboring tribes such as the Zuni, the Hopi, and the Pueblo.

The Navajo were **warriors** and **hunter-gatherers**. They knew little about farming. So, their Pueblo neighbors taught them how to grow corn, melons, beans, and squash. They also learned to **weave** cotton cloth.

Some settlers taught the Navajo how to make beautiful jewelry and blankets. The Navajo raided Spanish settlements for cattle, horses, and sheep.

A Navajo family tends sheep.

Homes

Navajo families lived in homes called hogans. Hogans were made of logs and rocks. They were framed in a circle about 30 feet (9 m) wide. The frames were covered with mud. It kept the hogans cool inside.

Each hogan had one door. The door faced east to greet the morning sun, which was **sacred** to the Navajo. A hole in the hogan's roof released smoke from the fire inside. Some hogans also had several outside shade shelters.

A shade shelter had a roof of sticks and bushes. Four or six posts held the roof up. It protected people, supplies, and tools from the sun and rain.

The Navajo often fixed their breakfast in the shade shelters. They would do some work there, too, such as making rugs. Sometimes, they just sat and talked.

A Navajo hogan

The wooden frame of a hogan

Food

Breakfast was ready by daybreak. Often it was **tortillas** and **mutton** stew. Roast mutton was another favorite food.

The main meals were usually vegetable and potato stews. Sometimes the stews had lamb, sheep, or goat meat in them. They were served with tortillas.

Corn, wheat, and vegetables were grown in the family fields. Women and children often gathered prickly pears, peaches, and **piñon nuts**. The women also gathered herbs and spices. They used these to make teas.

A Navajo woman tends to corn in her family's field.

Clothing

Men and women usually made their own clothes. When the Navajo first came to the desert, they wore deerskin clothes. Soon, their Pueblo neighbors taught them to **weave** cotton and wool cloth. Cotton and wool made better clothes for the hot climate. They kept people cooler than deerskin.

Women wore a dress called a *biil*. A *biil* was a blanket or large shawl. It had a slit in the middle. This allowed the head to slip through. The *biil* hung down past the knees. But it was open on both sides. The *biil* was gathered around the waist with a belt.

Men wore a shorter blanket or shawl. It, too, was gathered at the waist with a belt. Men also wore pants of woven cloth or deerskin.

OPPOSITE PAGE: A Navajo family in traditional dress. The man is wearing a shawl and woven pants. The woman is wearing a biil. She is holding an infant on a cradleboard.

Crafts

The Pueblo first taught the Navajo women how to **weave** blankets. The women wove beautiful blankets on **looms**. They placed different colored threads on the loom. These threads were woven tightly into beautiful patterns. As they worked, the women often sang songs.

Navajo men first learned to make silver jewelry from Mexican jewelers in the 1850s. The Navajo had only a few basic tools. But they created bracelets, necklaces, and belt buckles from silver dollars and **turquoise** stones.

Silver Navajo Rug
Design Cutout Earrings

Nellie Martin raises sheep, spins their wool into thread, and weaves it into rugs on her Navajo Nation farm near Navajo, New Mexico.

A black and white Navajo basket

A Navajo rug

15

Family

Navajo children were "born to" the mother's clan. This means the children took their mother's clan name. In this way, the Navajo traced their **ancestry**. This custom is still followed today.

When a young man married, it had to be to someone outside his clan. This rule is still observed today. Married people built their home near the bride's mother.

Women made most of the important family decisions. They owned the family's material possessions. Men respected women as possessors of wealth.

The Navajo lived in the countryside near their sheep. Sheep were the source of a family's wealth. Several related families built their hogans close together. The homes were often near a stream.

Navajo hogans near a stream

Children

Navajo children often grew up with many brothers, sisters, and cousins nearby. The older children guided the younger ones around the home and land as everyone worked.

A Navajo infant on a cradleboard watches a lamb approach.

Mothers, aunts, and grandmothers gave the children many tasks each day. Five- and six-year-olds carried water from the stream. They helped the **elders** cook, chop wood, and tend sheep.

Young girls learned to **weave** by watching their mothers. They helped pick the wild plants that made different colored dyes. The dyes colored the threads made from sheep's wool.

By the age of twelve or thirteen, girls had finished their first blanket. Fathers and uncles taught the boys to ride horses and work the sheep and cattle.

Navajo children tend crops and collect wood.

Medicine Man

Navajo medicine men often used sand paintings to help heal sick people. They poured thin lines of red, yellow, brown, or black sand from their hands. They created sand paintings to represent the illness affecting the sick person.

A Navajo sand painting

The sand was collected in different **sacred** places. Sand paintings were one to twenty feet (.3 to 6 m) across. Each took many hours to finish.

The medicine man sang songs as he dipped his hands in sticky plant juices. Then, he **anointed** the sick person. The sick person sat on the sand painting. Then, the medicine man sang songs about where the illness came from. When the healing ceremony was over, the sand painting was destroyed.

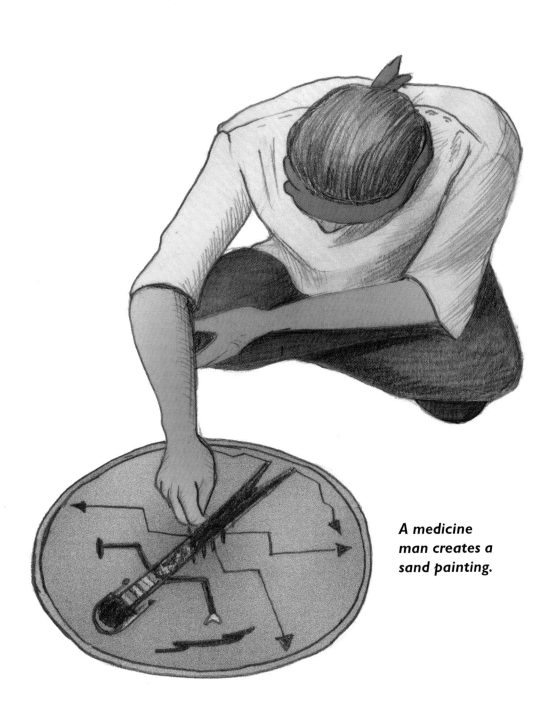

A medicine man creates a sand painting.

War

The Navajo were fierce **warriors**. When they first came to the desert, they fought the Pueblo, Ute, and Comanche for land. They also fought to protect their lands from Spanish, Mexican, and American forces during the 1800s.

During the Navajo War of 1863-66, the U.S. government forced the Navajo from their homelands. They marched to Fort Sumner in eastern New Mexico. This march is known as the "Long Walk of the Navajo."

Many of the **elders** and young children died on the march and at Fort Sumner. Some were too weak to make the journey. Others became ill or starved.

In 1868, the Navajo promised the U.S. government never to go to war again. They signed a treaty with the government. Then the government allowed the Navajo to return to their home.

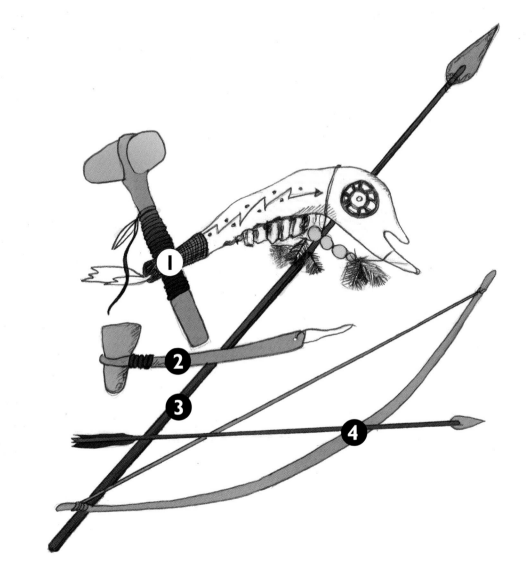

1. Navajo war clubs 2. Tomahawk. 3. Spear 4. Bow and Arrow

Contact with Europeans

Navajo pictographs of Spanish riders

A pueblo in New Mexico

In 1582, Spanish explorer Antonio de Espejo led his troops into the Navajo homelands from Mexico. It was the first time the Navajo had seen Europeans.

The Spanish described the Navajo as peaceful. The Navajo brought the explorers **tortillas** when they met.

The Spaniards made war on the Zuni, the Hopi, and the Pueblo. These tribes lived in big **pueblos**. There, they could be easily attacked.

The Navajo survived because they were harder to find. They could easily escape across the desert when an enemy approached. The Spaniards left them alone.

24

A Navajo warrior and a Spanish explorer meet for the first time.

Barboncito

In 1868, the U.S. government wanted to move the Navajo to a **reservation** in Oklahoma. Barboncito, one of the first Navajo leaders, talked the government officials into allowing the Navajo to stay on their homelands. He said to them:

"After we get back to our country, it will brighten up again. And the Navajos will be as happy as the land. Black clouds will rise. And there will be plenty of rain. Corn will grow in abundance. And everything will look happy."

Barboncito signed the last treaty between the Navajos and the United States on June 1, 1868. It established the original Navajo Reservation in the Chuska Mountains of Arizona. He died there three years later. The Navajos have prospered ever since.

Barboncito was a medicine man, war chief during the Navajo War of 1863-66, and head chief during the Treaty of 1868 signing.

The Navajo Today

In 1936, the U.S. government chose Window Rock, Arizona, as the site for the Navajo Central Agency. Today, Window Rock serves as the capital of the Navajo Nation.

There once was a spring under the rock. It was a place where the Navajo medicine men obtained water for ceremonies that were held to produce rain and cure illness.

The Navajo are the largest Native American tribe in the U.S. Over 200,000 live in the Navajo Nation in northern Arizona, Utah, and New Mexico.

The Tribal Council oversees the tribal government. The tribe sells the oil and mineral deposits on its lands. The tribe uses the money for the tribal government. Navajo arts and crafts are popular with collectors and museums worldwide.

Window Rock Natural Arch

An operating coal mine near Window Rock

Navajo Nation Council Chamber in Window Rock, Arizona

Two young Navajo boys sit in an oval-shaped rock opening in Black Rock Canyon, Arizona.

Nellie Martin raises sheep on her Navajo Nation farm near Navajo, New Mexico.

Having fun at Window Rock, Arizona

Learning to become
a medicine man

A Navajo family from
Flagstaff, Arizona,
wears traditional dress.

Native Americans perform
traditional dances during the
Navajo Nation Fair at Window Rock

Glossary

ancestry - a line of descent.

anoint - to smear or rub with liquids.

butte - a steep hill that has a flat top and stands alone.

cradleboard - a decorated flat board with a wooden band at the top that protects the baby's head.

elder - a person having authority because of age or experience.

hunter-gatherers - people who feed themselves solely by hunting and gathering food. Hunter-gatherers do not grow crops.

loom - a wooden frame that is used to weave cloth or blankets from thread.

mutton - the meat of an older sheep.

piñon nuts - seeds that grow on piñons, or pine trees.

pueblo - a Native American village of homes grouped together to form a large building. Pueblos are built of adobe and stone.

reservation - land set apart by the United States government for Native Americans to live on.

sacred - something worthy of respect.

tortilla - a corn pancake used by many Native American tribes.

turquoise - a clear blue or greenish-blue precious stone used in jewelry.

warriors - fighters.

weave - to alternate horizontal and vertical threads to create a cloth.

Web Sites

For general information about the Navajo, visit **http://www.navajos.com/** This site has resources and information on the Navajo Nation and Navajo people of Utah, Arizona, and New Mexico. It has articles, a national calendar of events, a travel guide, links to resources, and more.

The official Web site of the Navajo Nation is **http://www.navajo.org/**

The Navajo Times (**http://www.thenavajotimes.com/**) is the official newspaper of the Navajo people.

These sites are subject to change. Go to your favorite search engine and type in "Navajo" for more sites.

Index